CHAPLAINCY
AT THE CROSSROADS OF
CULTURE & CARE

M. C. BROWN

Crossroads Of Culture and Care

ISBN: 978-1-9192226-0-8

Published by:
MANIFEST R819 PUBLICATIONS
UK: +44204538872
USA: +1(347)749-8363
Email: admin@manifestr819.com
www.manifestr819.com

Crossroads Of Culture and Care

CONTENTS

Crossroads Of Culture and Care

4

Crossroads Of Culture and Care

Introduction

- Purpose of the book
- The unique lens of a Black African chaplain in a multicultural healthcare context
- The importance of cultural humility, sensitivity, and spiritual flexibility in end-of-life care
- The power of storytelling in shaping inclusive chaplaincy practice

Part I: The Chaplain's Identity and Calling
Chapter 1: Wearing the Collar, Bearing the Culture

- The experience of being a visible minority in NHS chaplaincy
- Navigating professional expectations and cultural self-awareness
- Trust, suspicion, and building credibility

Chapter 2: What Does a Chaplain Do? – Redefining Presence

- Dispelling myths about chaplaincy
- The difference between religious instruction and spiritual support
- Ministry of presence in culturally diverse spaces

Part II: End-of-Life Encounters Across Cultures and Faiths

Chapter 3: The Silent Son – End-of-Life in a Caribbean Family

- Cultural expressions of strength and silence
- Intergenerational differences in grief
- Creating sacred space in emotional restraint

Chapter 4: "My Mother Must Not Die in Pain" – A Nigerian Pentecostal Perspective

- High faith expectations around divine healing
- Tension between medical reality and spiritual hope
- The chaplain as interpreter and reconciler

Chapter 5: When the Imam Arrives – Working with Muslim Families

- Honour, modesty, and the presence of extended family
- Rituals at the moment of death
- Respecting Islamic practices within hospital protocols

Chapter 6: Rituals Interrupted – A Hindu Patient's Final Hours

- Cultural rituals disrupted by hospital schedules
- Supporting families through spiritual compromise
- Collaboration with staff for compassionate flexibility

Chapter 7: Dying Young – The Ghanaian Boy and a Shattered Dream

- Collective grief in African diaspora families
- Cultural understanding of death and destiny
- Empowering a family's grieving process

Part III: Reflections and Lessons in Cultural Humility

Chapter 8: When Belief and Biology Collide

- Faith declarations versus clinical diagnosis
- Ethical tensions in end-of-life faith conversations
- Chaplain as bridge, not judge

Chapter 9: Language of the Heart – Interpreting Beyond Words

- The use of mother tongue in prayer and blessing
- The emotional power of culturally familiar words
- Spiritual care when translation fails

Chapter 10: Dying in a Foreign Land

- The immigrant's fear of dying away from home

- Issues of identity, belonging, and funeral repatriation
- Supporting existential concerns

Part IV: Toward a More Inclusive Chaplaincy.

Chapter 11: Cultural Competence is Not Enough

- Moving from competence to cultural humility
- Unlearning biases and asking better questions
- Stories as tools for awareness and transformation

Chapter 12: When We Too Are Grieving – The Chaplain's Humanity

- The emotional toll of repeated exposure to death

- Navigating personal grief in professional spaces
- Self-care, supervision, and spiritual resilience

Conclusion: Dignity in Diversity

- Key themes and insights
- The future of chaplaincy in a multicultural NHS
- Encouragement for current and future chaplains

Appendices

- Glossary of cultural/religious end-of-life practices
- NHS and spiritual care guidance documents
- Reflection questions for chaplaincy students or practitioners

Crossroads Of Culture and Care

INTRODUCTION

T his book is born from the quiet corridors of NHS hospitals, where lives begin, heal, and end, often in silence, often in the presence of people who do not look, sound, or pray like each other. As a Black African chaplain working within this system, I have had the profound honour of accompanying people from vastly different backgrounds through the final chapters of their lives. In doing so, I have witnessed both the beauty and the complexity of multicultural and multi-faith end-of-life care in the UK.

The purpose of this book is not to present clinical research or institutional analysis. Rather, it is to offer stories, real, raw, and human, captured from the bedside. These are curated accounts, each chosen not for their drama but for the lessons they carry about presence, dignity, culture, and faith. The book is a companion to fellow chaplains, healthcare professionals, and anyone who cares about how we support people from diverse backgrounds in their final days. It is an invitation to listen deeply, to question assumptions, and to allow ourselves to be changed by what we witness.

THE UNIQUE LENS OF A BLACK AFRICAN CHAPLAIN IN A MULTICULTURAL NHS

Being a chaplain is already a calling that demands spiritual maturity, emotional resilience, and deep listening. Being a Black African chaplain in the NHS adds another layer.

I walk into rooms where I am sometimes the first chaplain a patient has seen, let alone one with African features, an accent, or a name unfamiliar to the British tongue. That visibility carries weight. At times, it disarms. At other times, it evokes surprise, discomfort, or even suspicion.

Yet it is precisely this intersection, of race, culture, and vocation, that offers a rich and unique lens into the lived experiences of patients and families who often find themselves unseen or unheard in clinical settings. I understand what it means to carry the expectations of one's community, to navigate multiple cultural identities, and to hold faith with both passion and complexity. I bring with me not just theological training, but the wisdom of elders, the rhythm of African grief, and the conviction that death is not the enemy, it is the final sacred encounter.

In a healthcare system that continues to grapple with structural inequalities and cultural misunderstandings, I have found that my identity is not a limitation, it is a bridge. It enables trust, empathy, and spiritual companionship across divides that might otherwise remain unspoken.

THE IMPORTANCE OF CULTURAL HUMILITY, SENSITIVITY, AND SPIRITUAL FLEXIBILITY IN END-OF-LIFE CARE

Culture shapes how we live, but it also profoundly shapes how we die. The rituals we expect, the language we use, the prayers we whisper, and the people we want near us, all of these are informed by our cultural, religious, and communal identity.

In the NHS, there is a growing awareness of the need for "cultural competence." But competence alone is not enough. What is required is cultural humility, a posture of

ongoing learning, of asking rather than assuming, of stepping back when the moment
calls for listening instead of leading. As chaplains, we are not just offering spiritual care,
we are offering spiritual safety. That means
being flexible, adaptive, and aware of the sacred scripts each person brings into the dying process.

This book explores how cultural expectations at the end of life can either be honoured
or unintentionally disrupted by hospital rou-
tines. Whether it is a Caribbean family's
quiet dignity, a Nigerian son's prophetic
prayer, a Muslim patient's burial rites, or a
Hindu daughter's need for ritual purity,
chaplaincy must be a space of welcome, not
erasure.

These stories are not about cultural perfor-
mance, they are about sacred meaning. And
if we fail to respect those meanings, we risk

adding distress to an already tender moment.

THE POWER OF STORYTELLING IN SHAPING IN-CLUSIVE CHAPLAINCY PRACTICE

Why stories? Because policies do not sit at the bedside. People do. And people are shaped not just by training or checklists, but by the stories that open their hearts and challenge their biases.

This book does not aim to offer every answer. Instead, it offers windows, into grief, resilience, anger, peace, and love. Each chapter presents a case, an encounter, a moment. And within those moments are questions:

- What does it mean to die with dignity in a culture not your own?
- How do we support faith that resists medical reality?
- How do we listen across language barriers and spiritual frameworks?

Stories disarm defensiveness. They human-
ise statistics. They remind us that behind
every bed number is a name, a family, a history, and a future that someone hoped
would be longer. For those of us in chaplaincy, storytelling also becomes part of our
own healing, because in telling the stories of
others, we make meaning out of the sorrow
we witness.

In each chapter, I invite you not just to read
but to pause. To ask: *What would I have done?*
What do I assume? What do I need to learn?

This book is not a complete catalogue of all
BAME experiences at the end of life. Nor
does it claim to represent all African or Black
British chaplains. Every story is unique,
shaped by personal history, theology, and
the specific dynamics of each ward or family.
What I offer here is a curated lens, honest,
personal, and reflective. Some experiences

will resonate deeply with those from African diasporic communities. Others will challenge readers to consider the limits of their own cultural understanding. And that is the point: not to generalise, but to broaden the conversation.

As I wrote these chapters, I was conscious of the delicate balance between protecting the confidentiality of those involved and telling their stories in ways that preserve their power. All names and identifying details have been changed. The truth of the encounters remains.

If you are a chaplain, this book is for you. If you are a nurse, a doctor, a social worker, or a hospital volunteer, this book is for you. If you are a person of faith seeking to understand how spirituality and culture shape the end of life, this book is for you. If you have ever sat at the side of someone dying, unsure of what to say or how to be present, this book is for you.

You do not need to agree with every theological insight or cultural interpretation presented here. What I hope you will agree with is the necessity of dignity, presence, and cultural respect in end-of-life care.

Because when the monitors go silent, the family gathers, and the final breath is taken, it is not just a medical moment. It is a human one. And how we handle that moment tells us everything about who we are as a society.

Chaplaincy sits at a crossroads, a place where culture meets care, where medicine meets mystery, where sorrow meets hope. It is not always a comfortable space. But it is a necessary one.

As a Black African chaplain, I do not bring all the answers. But I bring my presence, my prayers, my culture, and my commitment to hold space, especially when that space is complex, crowded, or confused.

This book is my offering. May it speak to the heart of your vocation, expand your understanding, and honour the sacred work we are privileged to do at the edge of life.

Let us stand together at the crossroads, with humility, with courage, and with compassion.

PART I:

THE CHAPLAIN'S IDENTITY AND CALLING

Crossroads Of Culture and Care

CHAPTER 1

WEARING THE COLLAR, BEARING THE CULTURE

"To be fully present at the bedside, I must first be at peace with who I am."

Being a Black African chaplain in the NHS is both an honour and a daily negotiation. I am called to offer spiritual support to people of all backgrounds, many of whom do not look like me, pray like me, or even understand what my presence means. I walk into rooms where I am often the first chaplain they have seen, let alone one with an African accent and skin the colour of the earth. In those moments, I do not just represent the chaplaincy service; I carry my race, my culture, and my calling on my shoulders.

Some see the collar and find comfort. Others see the colour and feel uncertainty. I have learned not to take first reactions personally. In fact, I have come to understand that the very things which make me different are often the things that make me most effective, if handled with humility and wisdom.

BRIDGING WORLDS: BETWEEN CULTURES AND EXPECTATIONS

In many African cultures, chaplains are understood primarily in religious terms, pastors who preach, pray, or lead services. But in the NHS, chaplaincy is broader and more inclusive. We are called to be a spiritual presence, regardless of a person's faith, culture, or worldview. This can sometimes cause tension, particularly within myself. How do I, as a committed Christian and African man, serve a patient who is Buddhist, atheist, or pagan? What do I do when I am called to be with someone who has no faith language at all?

At first, I struggled. I wondered whether I was compromising my faith or drifting into syncretism. But over time, I learned the deeper meaning of "presence", being with, without agenda. I discovered that God is already in the room, and I am there simply to help the patient or family encounter whatever peace, meaning, or closure they need in that moment. This has transformed how I see both my cultural identity and my ministry.

TRUST, SUSPICION, AND THE SLOW WORK OF ACCEPTANCE

There are moments of suspicion, some quiet, some loud. A white patient once asked me directly: "Are you qualified to do this kind of job here?" On another occasion, a nurse assumed I was part of the cleaning staff because of my uniform and skin colour. I have been mistaken for a visitor, for security, for anything but a chaplain. But then there are sacred moments, moments when my presence speaks volumes.

A Jamaican grandmother once took my hand as her son passed away and whispered, "I'm glad it's you here. You understand." She did not mean theology. She meant the shared rhythm of our cultural grief, the unspoken language of loss in Black communities, the ability to cry without needing to explain. That moment reminded me that acceptance is not always immediate, but when it comes, it is profound.

BECOMING A CHAPLAIN OF MANY CULTURES

Over time, I have come to realise that being a Black African chaplain in the NHS is not about fitting in; it is about being a bridge. My background gives me insight into the emotional vocabulary of many BAME patients, particularly those from African or Caribbean backgrounds. But it also challenges me to remain open, to constantly learn, adapt, and honour traditions that are not my own.

Every patient teaches me something new. From Muslim rituals to Sikh prayers, from Irish Catholic death rites to secular humanist reflections, I am a student at every bedside. And in learning from others, I become a better chaplain not just for "them", but for all.

I do not leave my Africanness at the hospital door. I walk in with it, but not to impose. Rather, to embody the truth that chaplaincy, like humanity, is richer when all stories are welcomed.

My accent, my skin tone, my upbringing, and my Christian faith, all of these inform how I see the world. But I have learned not to let them limit how I serve the world.

This chapter, this calling, is about walking humbly, with collar and culture intact, and choosing presence over power, listening over lecturing, and love over labels.

CHAPTER 2

WHAT DOES A CHAPLAIN DO? – RE-DEFINING PRESENCE

"You don't say much, but somehow I feel lighter after you leave." – A patient's parting words

When people ask what a chaplain does, the assumptions are often narrow. *"Do you only pray with people?" "Do you preach at patients?" "Are you here to convert me?"* In some settings, chaplains are expected to arrive with a Bible in hand and Scripture on the lips. In others, we

are avoided out of fear that we bring a religious agenda or bad news.

Yet the core of chaplaincy in the NHS is not
religious instruction, it is presence. Presence
that listens. Presence that sees. Presence that
sits in silence when words are too heavy. We
are there not simply to speak but to accompany, to hold space for the spiritual, emotional, and existential weight that patients
and families carry, especially at the end of
life.

• **Listening Without Fixing**

A woman once burst into tears the moment I
entered the ward. She had lost her child that
morning, and when she saw my chaplain's
badge, she said, "Oh, thank God, someone
who isn't here to take blood or ask questions." I did not offer a prayer. I did not quote

a Bible verse. I sat beside her. I listened. That was all she needed.

Chaplaincy at its best is not about having the right words; it is about being a compassionate, non-anxious presence. We do not come to fix grief. We come to bear witness to it.

Sometimes, the presence of someone who is not rushing, who is not clinical, who is not prescribing anything, is the most powerful support in the room. We become what some call a "sacred interruption", a moment in which someone is no longer a patient, but a person.

- **Beyond Faith Labels**

It is easy to assume chaplaincy is for religious people only. But some of my most meaningful encounters have been with those who tick "no religion" on their records. A middle-aged man dying of cancer once said, "I don't do God, but I do silence." We sat for twenty minutes in silence. Then he asked, "Do you think I've been a good man?" That was the doorway to a profound reflection, not on doctrine, but on legacy, on meaning, on forgiveness.

Spiritual care is broader than religion. It encompasses questions of hope, fear, belonging, guilt, love, and eternity. Whether a person is a devout Muslim, a lapsed Catholic, a questioning agnostic, or an atheist with spiritual wounds, the chaplain's role is to meet them where they are, not where we wish they were.

- **Faithful Without Being Forceful**

As a Christian chaplain, I carry my faith with me. It shapes my ethics, my compassion, and my desire to serve. But I do not carry it like a megaphone. Chaplaincy has taught me how to minister without domination. I have learned to pray in the way a patient understands, sometimes by asking, "What would be meaningful for you right now?" Sometimes the answer is a Scripture reading. Other times, it is simply a hand on the shoulder.

I remember a Sikh woman who was afraid of dying alone. I could not chant her sacred hymns, but I asked, "Would you like me to stay with you in silence?" She nodded. Before she passed, she opened her eyes and said, "You brought peace with you." That is chaplaincy.

- **The Power of Being With**

There is a ministry of *being* that is sometimes more powerful than *doing*. Sitting beside someone in silence. Holding the hand of a dying child's parent. Whispering words of peace into a room thick with fear. These are not headline moments, but they are holy ones.

Chaplains are trained to observe the unspoken, to discern the sacred in the ordinary, and to offer spiritual companionship without judgement or pressure.

In many African and BAME cultures, spiritual leadership is highly verbal, preaching, singing, commanding. However, in the healthcare context, the role of the chaplain requires a different kind of strength: the strength to be quiet, the courage to be still, and the wisdom to wait.

What does a chaplain do? We show up. We listen. We hold hands, hold hearts, and hold hope when others are losing theirs. We enter rooms not to bring answers, but to stand in the questions.

We are present. And sometimes, that is all a person needs to feel they are not alone.

PART II:

END-OF-LIFE ENCOUNTERS ACROSS CULTURES AND FAITHS

CHAPTER 3

THE SILENT SON – END-OF-LIFE IN A CARIBBEAN FAMILY

"Grief doesn't always cry out loud. Sometimes it sits in silence, heavy and holy."

The ward was unusually still that afternoon. The curtains had been drawn around the bed of an elderly woman, Mrs A., a Jamaican matriarch in her late eighties, who was nearing the end of her life. Her breathing was laboured but peaceful. Around her sat two daughters, one granddaughter, and a young man, the son.

41

He sat quietly in the corner, barely moving, barely speaking.

I had been called not to perform any rituals, but simply to *"be around the family"*, as one of the nurses had phrased it. This was one of those cases where nothing dramatic was happening, and yet, something sacred was unfolding.

The daughters spoke occasionally, reminiscing in soft Jamaican Patois about their mother's strength, her rice and peas, her church hat collection, and the way she used to correct them with just a look. But the son said nothing. He stared at the floor, hands clenched, emotion unreadable.

In some cultures, grief is expressive and vocal. In others, it is quiet, stoic, or even deferred. Caribbean families often grieve communally, but with a cultural strength that sometimes appears emotionally restrained, especially among men. The son's silence was not detachment. It was grief, guarded and internal.

This is where cultural sensitivity is essential. A chaplain unfamiliar with these dynamics might misread the silence as indifference or avoidance. But I knew better. I have seen the Caribbean ethos of dignity in grief, the way pain is sometimes carried privately to preserve a sense of control.

I did not press the son to speak. I did not ask the family invasive questions. I simply sat in the room, offering what I have come to call *"quiet ministry"*. I listened as the women spoke. I passed tissues when needed. I made gentle eye contact with the son, nodding in silent acknowledgment.

After some time, I offered a soft blessing over Mrs A. I asked if I could say a prayer for peace, and the family agreed. I prayed slowly, choosing words rooted in dignity and rest, language that resonated with Christian heritage without assuming that all present were religious.

The son looked up briefly during the prayer. His eyes glistened.

Just before I left the room, I touched the son lightly on the shoulder and said, "You're holding a lot. If you ever want to talk, I'm around."

He did not respond then, but hours later, as I was walking through the corridor, he found me. "Chaplain," he said, eyes red. "I didn't know what to say in there. She raised me. I just... I couldn't speak."

We found a quiet corner and sat together. He talked for thirty minutes about his grand-mother, his regrets, his fears of being the only male in the family now. He admitted he did not feel comfortable crying in front of the others.

"You don't have to cry in front of anyone," I told him. "But you also don't have to carry this alone."

He nodded slowly. "Thanks for not rushing me."

This encounter reminded me of an important truth: grief looks different in every culture and in every person. Some wail. Some laugh. Some go silent. The chaplain's role is not to normalise or interpret too quickly, but to re-main present long enough to understand what is really being communicated.

Caribbean expressions of grief are often layered with a cultural reverence for strength and control. This does not mean the grief is shallow, it often runs deep, shaped by faith, family, and ancestral pride. What looks like stoicism may, in fact, be a deeply spiritual surrender, an inner knowing that *"God knows, and He will take care of us."*

For BAME chaplains, and especially those from African backgrounds, supporting Caribbean families can feel both familiar and different. While we share a postcolonial heritage, Christian faith values, and strong family systems, there are subtle nuances, tones of language, gestures of respect, and gendered expectations, that require attentiveness.

In this case, knowing when not to speak was the ministry. Holding space for silence, honouring the son's quiet pain, and offering him time on his terms was far more effective than any prescribed grief counselling model.

Grief, in all its forms, deserves to be honoured, not interpreted too quickly, and never dismissed. For some, grief is a storm. For others, it is a slow river. As chaplains, we must learn the emotional landscapes of different cultures so we can walk alongside them, not as experts, but as fellow travellers on the sacred journey of letting go.

Crossroads Of Culture and Care

CHAPTER 4

"MY MOTHER MUST NOT DIE IN PAIN" – AN AFRICAN PENTECOSTAL PERSPECTIVE

"We serve a miracle-working God. This cannot be her portion."

I was called to the ward one evening to support a Nigerian family who had just been told that their elderly mother had only days, perhaps hours, to live. As I approached, the sound reached me before the sight did. I could hear the fervent, rhythmic voices of prayer rising from her bay.

The son, a tall, commanding man in his late forties, was pacing back and forth at the foot of her bed. His voice rang out in a mixture of English and tongues, the cadence of a seasoned intercessor. Every few steps, he declared a Scripture aloud: *"She shall not die, but live, and declare the works of the Lord!"*

The nurses had grown anxious. They stood at the edges of the bay, unsure how to intervene. He had refused morphine for his mother, insisting she would not need it because God was about to heal her. One nurse, glancing towards me, whispered, "He thinks prayer will stop her dying but she's in pain." This was not a moment for theological debate or clinical argument. This was a moment to step into the deep waters where faith, family, and fear converge, a space I know well, particularly within African Pentecostal contexts.

FAITH MEETS CLINICAL REALITY

For many West African Pentecostals, the language of faith is not gentle, it is militant. Death is cast as the enemy, to be defeated with spiritual warfare. Healing is not merely hoped for, it is expected. Words are understood to carry profound spiritual weight. To speak of dying is seen as giving death an invitation. And so, even when death is imminent, the declarations remain unyielding.

I knew this instinctively, not only as a chaplain, but as an African Pentecostal Charismatic minister. I had heard these same affirmations echoing in prayer meetings in Lagos, in revival tents in Accra, in modest UK church halls filled with fervent worshippers, and even at bedsides in my own extended family.

However, in the hospital environment, where clinical teams focus on comfort, dignity, and symptom management at the end of life, this defiant language can appear at odds with the medical goals of care. To staff unfamiliar with the culture, it can feel like obstruction, denial, or even aggression.

The real challenge was not to dismantle this man's theology in his moment of grief, but to gently reframe it, to help him see that accepting palliative measures was not faithlessness, but an expression of deep, compassionate love.

I introduced myself, my voice steady and respectful, and asked softly if we could step into the corridor. He hesitated, then agreed. "I know you believe God can heal," I began. He nodded firmly. "Of course. He is Jehovah Rapha, the Lord who heals. My mother has served Him all her life. This is not how her story ends."

"I understand," I replied gently. "But if this is her final chapter, what would it mean to give her peace in it?"

He paused, his gaze fixed but unblinking. The tension in his jaw was visible.

"She's in pain," I continued, keeping my tone calm. "Refusing pain relief will not make her live longer, but it may make her last hours harder. What if faith also means trusting God enough to ease her suffering?"

His eyes began to glisten. "I just… I don't want to let go."

And there it was, the truth behind the declarations. Not simply denial. Not arrogance. But love. Love wrapped in the language of faith. Grief cloaked in warfare prayers.

HOLDING SPACE FOR GRIEF IN FAITH COMMUNITIES

In many Pentecostal environments, particularly in African contexts, grief is rarely allowed to stand alone. Expressions of sorrow are often redirected into proclamations of victory. We do not mourn, we declare. We do not cry, we confess. Yet beneath these bold affirmations often lies unspoken sorrow, pressing heavily on the heart.

As chaplains, we must become skilled in listening between the lines, hearing the emotions buried under the theological language, and gently creating space for that emotional truth to surface without dishonouring the person's faith.

I asked if I could pray, not only for his mother, but with him. In that prayer, I wove together both faith and farewell. I called on

God's healing power, but also His comforting presence. I prayed for strength in the waiting, wisdom in the decisions, and the peace that passes all understanding.

When we returned to the room, his posture had softened. He gave the nurse a small nod, permitting her to administer morphine. Later, I saw him at his mother's bedside, holding her hand and softly singing her favourite hymn, a tender act of surrender in a man who had been braced for battle.

BRIDGING FAITH AND CARE

That day, I was reminded that faith and medicine are not natural enemies, but they do require a translator. The chaplain is often that translator, able to speak the language of spiritual hope in a way that is intelligible to medical teams, and to speak the language of clinical care in a way that feels acceptable to the faithful.

We are not called to extinguish hope, but to anchor it in love. To say, in both word and action: *God is still God, even when healing means letting go.*

Some battles are not won in the way we expect. For many African Pentecostal families, releasing a loved one into God's hands when every fibre of their theology cries out for a miracle is an act of immense courage.

Chaplaincy extends a sacred invitation in such moments: to trust that God's presence does not depart in death, that His care is not diminished when physical healing does not come, and that faith is not defeated when comfort is given.

Crossroads Of Culture and Care

CHAPTER 5

WHEN THE IMAM ARRIVES – WORKING WITH MUSLIM FAMILIES

"Death is not the end, but a return. What matters is how we prepare for the journey."

The call came mid-afternoon from the critical care ward. A Muslim patient, Mr Sayeed, a man in his late sixties, was nearing the end of life. His large extended family had begun to gather. Staff were becoming uneasy; the number of visitors had exceeded hospital policy, and emotions were running high.

I was asked to attend, not because the patient shared my faith, but because a chaplain was needed to facilitate cultural and religious understanding at a tense and tender moment.

When I arrived, the room was full. Sons, daughters, nieces, nephews. Some sat close to the bed, quietly reciting from the Qur'an in soft, rhythmic tones. Others were in quiet discussion, speaking in hushed Urdu about the next steps. And at the centre of it all lay Mr Sayeed, barely conscious, his breathing shallow, his face peaceful but pale. The family had already contacted the local Imam, who was on his way.

I understood my role clearly. I was not there to take the spiritual lead, but to offer emotional care, pastoral presence, and practical support. I was there to help ensure the family's needs were honoured, to mediate where necessary, and to uphold dignity during these final, sacred hours.

THE ROLE OF RITUAL IN DYING WELL

In Islamic tradition, death is not viewed as a tragic end but as a transition, a return to the Creator. It is a moment of profound spiritual significance, shaped by clear religious and cultural practices. The final words spoken over the dying are deeply important. The positioning of the body, the washing after death, and the speed of burial are all rooted in both faith and duty.

Many Muslim families wish for their loved ones to pass with the *Shahada*, the Islamic declaration of faith, either spoken by the dying person themselves or gently recited into their ear by a family member.

One of the sons approached me. His voice was respectful, but firm. "You are the chaplain, yes? We are waiting for the Imam, but please make sure no one moves his head or touches him unless it is absolutely necessary. And when he passes, we must be informed immediately, he must not be alone." This was not simply a request. It was an expression of religious responsibility, an urgent plea to protect what was sacred in their eyes. I reassured him that these wishes would be respected as far as possible within hospital policy.

Soon afterwards, the Imam arrived. He moved through the room with quiet authority, greeting the family and then nodding to me in warm acknowledgement. He stepped into the sacred space around the bed, and the room seemed to grow still.

Then came the recitation, deep, measured, melodic. The rhythmic beauty of the

Qur'anic verses filled the air, wrapping the moment in a sense of reverence. Some family members wept silently. Others closed their eyes, mouthing the words with him.

I stepped back towards the threshold, giving the Imam and the family full spiritual space, while remaining present to safeguard the atmosphere. My role became that of a quiet guardian, coordinating with nursing staff to limit interruptions, manage visitor flow, and protect the sacredness of what was unfolding.

When Mr Sayeed passed, it was with peace and dignity. The Imam continued reciting. The family wept, but their grief was anchored by acceptance. Within minutes, they were calmly discussing the funeral. For Muslims, burial is ideally conducted as soon as possible, often within 24 hours, so spiritual and practical preparations begin almost immediately.

LEARNING THE NUANCES

Supporting Muslim families at the end of life requires far more than a basic awareness of Islam. It calls for a sensitivity to detail, because details, in this context, are matters of spiritual obedience and honour. These include:

- **Gender boundaries** – Certain prayers or post-death rituals may be performed only by men or only by women, depending on tradition and family preference.
- **Privacy and modesty** – The patient's body must be treated with the utmost dignity, ideally by staff of the same gender where possible.
- **Language and leadership** – Many families defer to the Imam or to an elder for

all decisions, and chaplains must respect that chain of authority.

- **Burial timelines** – Any delay in paperwork or misunderstanding of hospital processes can cause profound distress to the family.

BUILDING TRUST THROUGH PRESENCE

Although I did not share their faith, the family later sought me out to thank me. One daughter said, "You didn't interfere, but you were there. You helped things go smoothly. That meant a lot."

Her words reminded me that interfaith chaplaincy is not about religious similarity, it is about relational solidarity.

My African Christian background did not disqualify me from walking alongside this Muslim family. On the contrary, my own cultural reverence for the dying allowed me to approach their moment with respect and empathy. Our rituals were different, but our understanding of death as sacred was the same.

When the Imam arrives, it is not the chaplain's time to take centre stage, it is a time to serve quietly. In such moments, the chaplain becomes a facilitator of dignity, a guardian of sacred space, and a partner in peace.

We do not need to know every verse, prayer, or custom. But we must carry enough humility to learn, enough wisdom to adapt, and enough compassion to protect what matters most. In this way, we honour both the faith of the family and the humanity we all share.

CHAPTER 6

RITUALS INTERRUPTED – A HINDU PATIENT'S FINAL HOURS

"When tradition is broken by circumstance, grief often finds no place to rest."

I was paged urgently to the oncology ward. A Hindu woman, Mrs P., aged seventy-two, was actively dying. Her family had just been told that she had only a few hours left. Emotions were running high. The eldest son had become visibly agitated with the nursing staff, complaining that they were "disrupting everything", while his sisters tried, unsuccessfully, to calm him down.

When I arrived, I was met with a scene of confusion and desperation.

"Chaplain," one of the nurses said, "they're asking for some kind of ritual or priest. But the family priest isn't answering, and they don't know what to do. They want the body turned, water placed in the mouth, incense lit, we're not sure how to respond."

This was not merely about religion, it was about a deeply ingrained cultural ritual of release. A sacred tradition was under threat, hemmed in by institutional time limits, clinical restrictions, and the absence of the right spiritual leader.

THE POWER OF RITUAL AT THE TIME OF DEATH

In many Hindu traditions, the final moments before death are profoundly sacred. The rituals surrounding this time are intended to support the soul's (*atman*) journey from the physical body into its next phase, whether that be rebirth or union with the divine.

Some of the most common practices include:

- Placing a few drops of *Ganga Jal* (holy water from the River Ganges) into the mouth of the dying person.

- Chanting sacred mantras such as *Om Namah Shivaya* or verses from the *Bhagavad Gita*.

- Positioning the head of the patient to face east, symbolising alignment with the rising sun and spiritual auspiciousness.

- Lighting incense and ensuring the presence of family to chant and sing during the passing.

However, in a modern healthcare setting, these rituals can be significantly disrupted. Fire alarms prohibit incense. Water at the bedside may pose safety risks. Space is shared with other patients. These limitations, while necessary for safety, can leave families feeling as though their loved one's passing is incomplete, creating a lingering sense of spiritual disconnection and unresolved grief.

STANDING IN THE GAP

Seeing the family's distress, I asked if I could sit with them. Though I am not Hindu, I approached with deep reverence.

"Would you like to share with me what's most important right now?" I asked the son. He exhaled heavily. "She must go in peace. We need to say the prayers. We need to do it right." "Would it help," I asked gently, "if we created as much space as possible for those prayers here, while working within the ward's safety rules?" He nodded slowly. "Yes, if we could just do something."

Together with the nurse in charge, we found a way forward. A small container of water, representing the sacred Ganges, was brought in and placed respectfully on the table near Mrs P.'s bed. The eldest daughter began to chant softly, her voice trembling yet resolute. Though incense could not be lit, we dimmed the lights and closed the curtain to create a sense of privacy and sacredness. I stood nearby in silent support, not as a priest, but as a protector of the space they were trying to preserve.

<u>CULTURAL PAIN AND INSTITUTIONAL BOUNDA-RIES</u>

What unfolded in that small bay was sacred, not because every ritual was perfectly executed, but because the heart of the tradition was honoured. Mrs P. passed away peacefully, surrounded by the voices and love of her children.

Afterwards, the son approached me. "Thank you for not rushing us," he said quietly. "Thank you for understanding, even if you are not Hindu."

His words underscored a profound truth: cultural grief deepens when sacred rituals are denied or truncated. For many South Asian families, end-of-life is far more than a biological transition, it is a spiritual crossing. It must be marked with dignity, order, and devotion. When these elements are disrupted, the grief that follows can feel incomplete, as though something essential has been left undone.

LESSONS FOR CHAPLAINS AND CARE TEAMS

This experience reinforced for me that chaplains are often called to be more than silent companions. Sometimes we are advocates, helping clinical teams understand the spiritual and emotional consequences of interrupting or modifying rituals.

Practical guidance includes:

- **Ask, don't assume.** Families may not know what is permitted. A simple, respectful conversation can open the way for creative compromises.
- **Collaborate with nursing staff.** Many are willing to make accommodations if the significance is explained clearly and early.
- **Hold the sacred space.** Even when the correct religious leader is unavailable, the chaplain's calm presence can help families feel grounded and supported.

An interrupted ritual does not necessarily mean a failed one. Sometimes the deepest sacredness emerges not from perfection, but from adaptation, when the heart of the tradition is preserved despite the limits of circumstance.

When chaplains bring humility, cultural sensitivity, and a willingness to negotiate respectfully with clinical systems, even a partial expression of a ritual can bring profound peace.

Mrs P. died with dignity. Her family grieved her loss, but also found comfort in the fact that their tradition, though incomplete, was still upheld in essence. In that fragile space between loss and longing, I was reminded that chaplaincy is not about being everything to everyone. It is about standing beside people as they do what they must do to say goodbye.

CHAPTER 7

DYING YOUNG – THE GHANAIAN BOY AND A SHATTERED DREAM

"He was supposed to graduate, not be buried."

It was just past seven o'clock in the morning when I received the call. A Ghanaian teenager, Kwaku, had been rushed into the intensive care unit overnight following sudden complications from a chronic illness. His condition had deteriorated rapidly, and his family had just been told there was nothing more the medical team could do. They were in shock, and the nursing staff believed that a chaplain's presence would help.

When I arrived at the family room, I was met by a wall of grief.

Kwaku's parents, both immigrants from Ghana, sat together on the hospital couch, motionless and disoriented. His younger sister clung desperately to her mother, sobbing uncontrollably. An uncle paced the corridor, speaking into his phone in Twi, coordinating urgent calls to extended family members across London and Ghana.

The father, his eyes red and swollen with grief, looked up at me and said quietly, "He just turned seventeen. He was supposed to go to university next year..."

I sat down beside them, saying nothing at first. In moments like these, silence can speak more deeply than words.

Crossroads Of Culture and Care

A DREAM DEFERRED, A FUTURE LOST

Kwaku's parents had arrived in the United Kingdom nearly two decades earlier, determined to build a better future for their children. He was their pride, top of his class, a football enthusiast, faithful at church, and loved by his peers. His sudden decline felt not only like a personal loss but like a cultural and generational collapse.

In many African communities, the death of a child or teenager is seen not only as a tragedy but as a profound rupture in the fabric of hope. Children carry not only our blood but our aspirations. They are living proof that the sacrifices of parents and grandparents meant something tangible. When one dies, the unspoken question hangs heavily in the air: *Was it all for nothing?*

THE SPIRITUAL WEIGHT OF CULTURAL GRIEF

As I listened to Kwaku's family, I recognised a grief I have seen many times in African households, a complex mixture of faith and questions, pride and devastation, strength and complete collapse.

The mother kept repeating, "God is not wicked, I know He is not wicked," as if saying it often enough might convince her heart of a truth her soul was struggling to accept.

The father alternated between numb silence and bursts of anguish: "I prayed! We fasted! We paid our tithes faithfully! How can this be?"

They were not angry at God in the traditional sense; rather, they were bewildered. They had done "everything right" according to their understanding of faith, and now they faced an outcome for which they were spiritually unprepared.

As a Black African chaplain, I knew instinctively that this was not the time for theological explanation or correction. What they needed was permission to lament—to pour out their pain without being told to cover it with declarations of faith.

NAMING THE PAIN, HONOURING THE LOSS

When the doctor confirmed that Kwaku had passed, the wailing began. His mother collapsed into my arms. His father wept openly. Yet amid the flood of grief, something deeply significant occurred.

The uncle called for prayer. He turned to me and said, "Please, man of God, lead us. He must not go without prayer."

I stood in the centre of that small room, surrounded by broken hearts, and prayed, not for healing, but for peace. I prayed for the release of Kwaku's spirit, for comfort to envelop his grieving family, and for the God they had trusted all their lives to meet them in their sorrow, not with explanations, but with His presence.

That prayer became a turning point. It did not end their pain, but it marked the beginning of communal mourning and the slow, sacred work of spiritual processing.

THE ROLE OF COMMUNITY AND THE AFRICAN EXTENDED FAMILY

Within an hour, more relatives began to arrive, cousins, elders, family friends, and members from their church. In African culture, grief is never borne alone. It is shared, embodied, and expressed together. People bring food, sing songs, pray aloud, and tell stories. The weight of loss is lightened by the number of hands and hearts carrying it.

But within a hospital setting, this cultural mourning often comes into conflict with policy. Visiting restrictions, space limitations, and clinical expectations can make families feel as though their expressions of grief are too loud, too numerous, and too disruptive. As a chaplain, I have often found myself advocating for *space*, not only physical space, but cultural space. I explain to hospital staff that for many African families, mourning is not silent. It is vocal, prayerful, physical, and infused with spiritual ritual. What may feel overwhelming to some is profoundly healing to others.

Kwaku's death was a sobering reminder that chaplains do not only support those who are dying, we also support the dreams that die with them. In his passing, his parents lost not just a beloved son, but a vision of the future they had sacrificed so much to secure.

In the weeks that followed, I continued to visit them, sometimes to pray, sometimes simply to sit in silence, and sometimes to listen as they shared stories and tears.

This is the work of end-of-life chaplaincy: not fixing broken hearts, but witnessing them. Not explaining away grief, but holding space for it. Not ending mourning, but helping it move.

Kwaku's story remains with me. It reminds me that while we cannot preserve every life, we can always honour every loss, especially when that loss carries the weight of generations.

PART III:

REFLECTIONS AND LESSONS IN CULTURAL HUMILITY

CHAPTER 8

WHEN BELIEF AND BIOLOGY COL-LIDE

"She's not dying, she's just sleeping. God will wake her."

In a quiet side room of the hospital's stroke ward, I encountered a scene I have witnessed many times in different forms. A young woman lay in a coma, her brain severely damaged. The medical team had done all they could, and the prognosis was unequivocal: she was not going to recover.

But gathered around her bed, her family remained convinced that healing was not only possible, it was imminent.

They were fervent believers, Pentecostal Christians originally from Zimbabwe. They prayed over her day and night, laid hands on her, and refused to speak of death.

"We reject that report," her sister told the doctor firmly. "Only God has the final say."

The doctor, though compassionate, was clearly growing frustrated. In a quiet aside, he told me, "We need to prepare the family for what's coming. But they're not engaging with the reality."

That is when chaplaincy is often called to do its most delicate work, navigating the collision between belief and biology.

FAITH THAT DEFIES THE FACTS

In many African Christian traditions, particularly in Pentecostal and charismatic circles, faith is expressed as certainty in the face of crisis. Scriptures are not merely recited as hopeful encouragement; they are declared as divine guarantees. Death is spoken of as defeat, and healing is claimed as a covenant right.

This belief system can provide immense strength, it can inspire resilience, perseverance, and even, on occasion, unexpected recovery. Yet it can also create deep internal conflict when medical outcomes fail to align with spiritual expectations.

I have heard statements like:

- "If we believe hard enough, she will wake up."
- "This is just a test. We must not speak negative things."
- "God is using this to show His glory."

I deeply respect such faith; I have seen it sustain families through unimaginable hardship. But I have also seen it become a barrier to acceptance, and at times, a breeding ground for guilt, when those left behind feel they must have "failed" in believing hard enough.

THE CHAPLAIN'S TIGHTROPE

As a chaplain, and as a fellow believer, I could understand both sides. The family's spiritual convictions were heartfelt and unshakeable. The medical team's assessment was clear and evidence-based. My place was in the space between hope and truth, belief and biology.

It was not my role to "choose a side" but to help the family hold space for both their faith and the reality unfolding before them. I sat with the parents in a quiet room and asked, gently: "What would it mean if healing looks different from what we are expecting?" They looked at me, puzzled.

"What if God is answering, but in a way we had not planned? What if peace is also a kind of healing?"

There was silence. Then the father exhaled slowly. "But we cannot give up."

I nodded. "Faith is not giving up. Sometimes it is trusting that even in death, God is still good."

That exchange opened a door, not a wide one, but just enough to allow the possibility of acceptance to enter alongside their hope.

THE POWER OF PASTORAL TRANSLATION

Much of chaplaincy in these moments is translation, not of spoken language, but of worldview.

- Translating medical facts into spiritually digestible truths.
- Reframing death not as defeat, but as transition.

- Showing that stopping aggressive treatment is not surrendering faith, but embracing compassion.

Sometimes I use Scripture, carefully, with pastoral sensitivity. "Even Jesus wept," I remind them. "And in Gethsemane, He prayed for another way, but then said, 'Not my will.' That too is faith."

This is not about undermining belief. It is about broadening the understanding of what faith can look like at the end of life.

STAFF MISUNDERSTANDINGS AND CULTURAL DISCONNECT

For healthcare staff unfamiliar with African Christian traditions, such expressions of faith can be misunderstood, as denial, delusion, or resistance. But in reality, they are often an integral part of the spiritual coping process, deeply rooted in a worldview where the spiritual realm is seen as more real than the physical.

I have said to nurses:

- "Give them time. This is how they process grief."
- "Let's not rush them into acceptance, grief has its own spiritual language."

Such conversations can build bridges between medical teams and families, fostering empathy and avoiding unnecessary conflict.

When belief and biology collide, the chaplain's role is to stand in that sacred gap, not to resolve it, but to hold it with compassion. To honour the family's faith without dismissing clinical truth. To help the heart catch up to what the body already knows.

In doing so, we discover that faith does not always need to be "fixed", it needs to be heard, respected, and gently expanded.

And in that delicate dance between hope and letting go, chaplaincy becomes what it is meant to be: not the bringer of all the answers, but the faithful companion in life's deepest mysteries.

CHAPTER 9

LANGUAGE OF THE HEART – INTER-PRETING BEYOND WORDS

"I didn't understand what you said, but I understood what you meant."

I walked into the room of an elderly woman from Eritrea, nearing the end of her life. Her daughter had asked for a chaplain. "She doesn't speak much English," she explained, "but she's afraid. Maybe you can pray with her?"

I greeted the woman gently, beginning with a few phrases in English. When I saw that my words were not connecting, I shifted to a slower, quieter presence, smiling, holding her gaze, using gestures of reassurance and peace. Then I offered a brief prayer aloud, my tone soft and calm.

She did not understand the literal meaning of the words, but her eyes softened. She closed them and placed her hand on her chest. She did not need a translation, she needed connection. In that moment, I was reminded that not all spiritual communication depends on a shared language. Sometimes tone, warmth, touch, or even silence can carry the message most powerfully.

BEYOND ENGLISH: THE LANGUAGE BARRIER IN END-OF-LIFE CARE

Within the NHS, many patients from migrant and ethnically diverse backgrounds encounter language barriers, especially in later life, when cognitive decline or emotional distress may cause them to revert to their native tongue.

At the end of life, people often instinctively reach for the language of their childhood, the language in which they first learned to pray, sing, cry, and express love.

In a clinical setting, this can create a profound disconnect. Patients may feel isolated, misunderstood, or unable to express their deepest needs. Staff, in turn, may misinterpret their behaviour, overlook subtle cues, or feel powerless to respond.

In such moments, chaplains often become not only interpreters of faith but also interpreters of emotion.

THE SOUND OF HOME

I remember sitting with a dying Somali grandmother who was restless and visibly agitated. The nurses had tried everything to calm her. Then a Somali porter, passing by, heard her faint muttering. He stepped into the room, spoke to her gently in Somali, and instantly, she relaxed. That single moment of familiar language restored her dignity.

Inspired by experiences like this, I now try to learn basic greetings and spiritual phrases in as many community languages as possible, simple yet profound words such as, "Peace be upon you," "God is near," or "You are not alone." Even when I cannot speak the language fluently, I ask family members:

- "What words or prayers would comfort them?"
- "What songs or hymns did they love at home or in worship?"

Sometimes, a family member will sing a familiar lullaby or hymn, and the dying person will respond with a tear, a smile, or a deep sigh. That is not mere sentiment, it is soul recognition.

THE BODY SPEAKS TOO

When words fail, the body continues to speak, through facial expressions, touch, posture, and breathing patterns. As chaplains, we are trained to listen to these unspoken cues:

- A furrowed brow may signal anxiety.
- A held breath may reveal fear.
- A relaxed hand may indicate readiness and peace.

I once sat with a dying Polish man who had refused all clergy visits. Yet his eyes kept drifting to the rosary beads lying on his bedside table. I picked them up and placed them gently in his hand. He wept silently.

That was ministry, without a single word exchanged.

CULTURAL ATTUNEMENT AND EMOTIONAL INTELLIGENCE

In many BAME communities, especially among elders, emotions are often conveyed with subtlety. Language barriers are only part of the challenge. Some people may not have the vocabulary to describe their emotional states in English, while others may hold back due to privacy, pride, or past trauma.

Chaplains must therefore become emotionally bilingual, fluent in empathy, fluent in silence, fluent in presence. This demands patience, observation, and deep respect. We do not rush to fill the silence. We do not impose our words. We allow the person to lead, even if their leadership comes through a whisper, a look, or the grasp of a hand.

At the end of life, fluency is not the primary need. What matters most is the feeling of being heard, seen, and honoured, even when illness or language has locked the words away. As chaplains, our calling is not merely to speak, but to listen with our hearts, to watch with spiritual attentiveness, and to respond with gentle presence.

For in the final hours, the language of the heart speaks most clearly, and it is this language that transcends all others.

CHAPTER 10

DYING IN A FOREIGN LAND

"I never thought I would die so far from home."

Mr Adewale, an elderly Nigerian man in his late seventies, had been living in the United Kingdom for nearly three decades. Yet, in his final days, all he longed for was to return home. "They must not bury me here," he told me, his voice weak yet resolute. "My bones belong to Ibadan."

It was not the first time I had heard such a plea. For many immigrants, particularly those from African, Caribbean, and South

Asian backgrounds, the wish to return home to die is deeply rooted in cultural identity, ancestral tradition, and a longing for closure. Yet, in reality, few ever make that final journey. The costs are high, the time is short, and the health risks are too great. As chaplains, we are often called to accompany people who are facing not only physical death, but also the emotional loss of a home they never stopped missing.

THE SOUL'S GEOGRAPHY

Home is more than a physical location. It is a feeling, a memory, and, for some, a belief that to die there is to die with dignity.
For Mr Adewale, dying in the United Kingdom felt like being cut off from all that was familiar:

- The language and sounds of his village
- The red earth beneath his feet

- The burial rites performed by his community
- The presence of extended family and elders who would honour him in the way he had always imagined

Lying in a London hospital bed, surrounded by machines and strangers, he felt a deep sense of spiritual dislocation. He belonged to this place in one sense, yet he did not feel at home in it.

"I came here for a better life," he whispered. "But this is not the land where I wanted to rest."

EXILE AT THE END

For many within diaspora communities, dying in a foreign land feels like a form of exile, even when they have spent most of their lives there. The landscape of their soul remains tied to the places of their youth, their ancestors, and their spiritual upbringing.

This dissonance can surface in various ways:

- Requests for the repatriation of the body
- Restlessness, despair, or agitation in the final days
- Expressions of longing for "the village", "the family house", or "my people"
- Spiritual unease or fear that they will not be "received properly" in death

I recall one Caribbean patient telling me, *"They won't know what to do with me here. Back home, they would sing me out."*

That single sentence carried layers of sorrow. He was not merely mourning his death; he was mourning the loss of ritual, recognition, and rootedness, elements that formed part of his identity.

CREATING HOME WHERE THERE IS NONE

As chaplains, we cannot always grant a dying person's wish to return home. But we can help bring a sense of home to them, through prayer, music, language, ritual, and the familiarity of culture.

With Mr Adewale, I asked gently: "Would it bring you peace if I called someone from your village or church back home to pray with you on the phone?"

His eyes lit up. We made the call, and I held the phone to his ear as an elder from his hometown prayed in Yoruba and sang an old hymn from his youth. Tears rolled down his cheeks.

Later, his daughter told me, *"That meant more to him than anything else the hospital could have done."*

THE ROLE OF REPATRIATION AND BURIAL RITES

In some cases, families will go to extraordinary lengths to send the body back to the country of origin. This, too, is sacred work. It is about honouring the wishes of the deceased and reconnecting death with ancestral soil.

Chaplains can support this process by:

- Advocating for prompt death certification and accurate documentation
- Working alongside bereavement teams to liaise with embassies, airlines, or community leaders
- Helping families navigate what is logistically and legally possible

Even when repatriation is not feasible, small acts, such as playing native music, reading prayers in the first language, or surrounding the bedside with familiar cultural symbols, can offer profound comfort.

To die in a foreign land is to face death as a stranger. And yet, chaplaincy can help restore a sense of belonging in those final hours. We can help the dying to feel seen, rooted, and honoured, even when they are far from the soil they call home.

Home, ultimately, is not only about geography. It is about being known, being remembered, and being blessed within the story that shaped you.

If we, as chaplains, can help create that sense of home at the end of life, then we have done the sacred work of making exile feel just a little more like home.

PART IV:

TOWARD A MORE INCLUSIVE CHAPLAINCY

Crossroads Of Culture and Care

CHAPTER 11

CULTURAL COMPETENCE IS NOT ENOUGH

"You can learn my customs and still not understand my pain."

BEYOND THE CHECKLISTS

In many healthcare settings today, *cultural competence* has become the buzzword of choice. Staff are trained to respect differences, use interpreters, consider dietary laws, and accommodate basic faith practices. Hospitals organise diversity training sessions and circulate leaflets outlining the essentials of world religions. These are good and necessary steps.

111

However, in my experience as a chaplain, particularly as a Black African chaplain working with Black, Asian, and Minority Ethnic (BAME) communities, I have come to recognise something crucial: cultural competence, on its own, is not enough.

It is one thing to know what to do. It is quite another to understand *why* it matters, *how* it feels, and *when* it is better to remain still rather than to assume understanding.

What patients and families often need at the end of life is not merely textbook knowledge. They need emotional intelligence, humility, and the willingness to sit with difference without rushing to "fix" it.

THE LIMITATIONS OF "LEARNING ABOUT"

Cultural competence, as it is often practised, tends to reduce people into broad categories:

- Muslims pray five times a day.
- Hindus prefer cremation.
- African families are expressive in grief.
- Asian families are family-oriented.

These statements may be statistically accurate, yet they fail to capture the nuance and complexity of lived experience.

I have met African families who grieve silently and white British families who wail openly. I have supported Christian families who decline prayer, and Muslim patients who request hymns.

Culture is not static; it is dynamic, layered, and deeply personal. People are not checklists, they are stories. To truly serve them, we must go beyond the generic and enter into the specific realities of the individual.

CULTURAL HUMILITY: A BETTER POSTURE

If cultural competence is about knowledge, cultural humility is about posture. It says:

- *"I don't know everything about your culture, but I am willing to learn."*
- *"You are the expert in your own story, I am here to listen."*
- *"I will not assume. I will ask. And I will adapt."*

As chaplains, this means entering every encounter as a learner rather than an authority. We leave space for the patient or family to shape the spiritual encounter, define what is sacred, and even correct our assumptions.

It also requires honesty about our own lenses. I carry African Christian perspectives that inevitably shape how I interpret silence, prayer, suffering, and grief. If I am not careful, I might project these interpretations onto others, assuming they see the world as I do. Cultural humility keeps me alert to my own biases.

LISTENING TO WHAT'S NOT SAID

Cultural humility also includes the ability to hear what is unspoken:

- A Caribbean grandmother saying, *"I'm fine"* may be concealing deep fear.
- A South Asian father who refuses pain medication may be expressing a deeply held value of stoic endurance.
- A Ghanaian Pentecostal declaring, *"She will not die"* may be wrestling privately with the reality of impending loss.

In such moments, I have learnt to ask gentle, open-ended questions that invite fuller truth:

- *"What would bring you peace right now?"*
- *"What is most important to your family in moments like this?"*
- *"Are there prayers, songs, or rituals that would bring you comfort?"*

These questions are invitations to stories, not summaries. They allow the person to speak from the heart, rather than to fit into a cultural script we have pre-written for them.

CHALLENGING INSTITUTIONAL BLIND SPOTS

Healthcare institutions often prefer neat categories and quick assessments. But real people rarely fit into tidy boxes.

I have sat in meetings where hospital staff expressed frustration with "difficult" families, often from BAME backgrounds, who were described as "too many, too loud, too resistant." What was missing in these conversations was the lens of cultural humility.

Were they loud because they were disrespectful, or because collective, vocal expression is their way of honouring the dead? Were they resistant because they were stubborn, or because they were navigating hospital rituals that felt alien and rushed compared to their own traditions?

Chaplains are uniquely placed to advocate for such families, not by excusing harmful behaviour, but by helping the institution understand the deeper values behind their actions. Cultural humility requires moving institutions beyond tolerance, towards genuine respect, where difference is not merely managed as a problem, but welcomed as a human reality.

FROM COMPETENCE TO CONNECTION

In the end, what every person approaching the end of life desires is not cultural perfection. They long for connection. They want to be seen, heard, and honoured, on their terms.

Competence may open the door; humility allows us to remain in the room. Humility enables us to listen without judgement, to honour without controlling, and to support without assuming.

As a Black African chaplain in the NHS, I have learnt many things. But I have also had to unlearn much: unlearn the belief that being the most knowledgeable automatically makes me the most effective; unlearn the assumption that shared ethnicity always means shared understanding; and unlearn the reflex to speak when silence might be the most sacred offering.

Cultural humility is not a destination, it is a lifelong journey. It is a commitment to keep learning, keep asking, and keep listening. Because in chaplaincy, as in life, the most powerful ministry is not the one that claims to know everything, but the one that makes space for others to be fully themselves.

Crossroads Of Culture and Care

CHAPTER 12

WHEN WE TOO ARE GRIEVING – THE CHAPLAIN'S HUMANITY

"You're the chaplain, you must be used to this."
Yes, but I am also human.

People often assume that chaplains are somehow immune to grief, that we have developed emotional calluses from being around death so frequently. They imagine we pray, comfort, and then move on, untouched by the pain that surrounds us. After all, we are the "strong ones," are we not?

121

The truth is, chaplains grieve too. We carry our own sorrows whilst holding space for the sorrows of others. We attend to death daily, sometimes multiple times in a single shift. And though we may not always show it in public, each loss leaves its mark.

There are patients we never forget. Families who remain etched in our hearts. Words that echo in our minds long after the ward round is over. Our calling does not make us less human, it exposes us more deeply to the fragility of life.

GRIEF BY ACCUMULATION

Unlike nurses or doctors who may focus on a specific condition or task, chaplains are often present for the entirety of the emotional and spiritual journey, from diagnosis to death, from moments of hope to moments of despair, from silence to final farewells. We do not merely witness the biology of dying, we witness its meaning.

This means our grief is often layered and cumulative. It does not always arrive as a single, overwhelming event. More often, it builds quietly over time:

- The young father who died leaving three small children.
- The grandmother who reminded us of our own.
- The refugee who died alone, far from home.
- The patient who was our age, or from our tribe, or shared our faith.

Each story we enter leaves behind a trace of sorrow mingled with compassion. Left untended, these traces can accumulate until they quietly overwhelm us.

WHEN THE PERSONAL MEETS THE PROFES-
SIONAL

There are times when our professional re-
sponsibilities collide with personal wounds.
I remember supporting a family who had
lost their teenage son in a road accident. He
was Ghanaian, just like me. His parents reminded me so vividly of my own that I felt
my heart ache with a familiarity I could not
ignore. As I prayed with them, tears pressed
against the back of my eyes, but I swallowed
them, telling myself, *"This is not about me."*

Yet when I arrived home that night, I broke
down. The grief I had contained in the hospital found its way into my private space, and
I could no longer hold it back.

These moments remind us of a truth that is
both humbling and necessary: we cannot

serve others well if we continually deny our own humanity.

SELF-CARE IS NOT SELFISH

In the African context, particularly among clergy, there is often an unspoken expectation to be endlessly strong. We are trained to *"stand in the gap,"* to carry the burden, to be unwavering spiritual anchors. But chaplaincy demands something different. It demands a willingness to be vulnerable, balanced with the self-awareness to care for our own wellbeing.

Self-care for chaplains is not indulgence; it is survival. It includes:

- Regular supervision or reflective practice.
- Debriefing with trusted colleagues.
- Time away from environments of trauma and sorrow.

- Prayer, meditation, or personal therapy.
- Setting healthy emotional boundaries without closing the heart.

We cannot pour from an empty cup. Nor should we attempt to.

PERMISSION TO FEEL

One of the most liberating truths I have learnt is this: we can be both caregivers and grievers. It is not weakness to feel, it is proof that our hearts remain open.

There are times I have cried after a shift. Times I have prayed, not for others, but for myself. Times I have lit a candle alone in the hospital chapel, not as the chaplain on duty, but as a soul in need of comfort.

These practices do not diminish my role. They deepen my integrity. For the most effective chaplain is not the one who remains outwardly unshaken, but the one who knows grief intimately enough to walk alongside others without judgement or fear of its weight.

As chaplains, we tread a delicate line, present for others in their darkest hours, yet often solitary in our own. The patients go home. The families leave. The wards fall silent. And we remain, carrying stories, sacred moments, and sorrows in the quiet spaces of our hearts. But we are not invincible. We are not divine. We are human beings called to holy work. And in that calling, we must also make space for our own mourning, our own healing, and our own humanity.

To be a chaplain is not to escape grief, it is to companion it, both in others and in ourselves.

CONCLUSION

DIGNITY IN DIVERSITY

"Every death is a sacred story. Every culture carries a sacred key."

This book has not been intended as an exhaustive account of chaplaincy work, nor could it ever be. Instead, it has offered a curated reflection: a journey through stories that have left an indelible mark on me, and which I believe hold profound meaning for the wider conversation about end-of-life care, cultural sensitivity, and spiritual support within the NHS.

As a Black African chaplain, I have stood at the bedsides of the dying from many nations, faiths, and walks of life. In every encounter, one unchanging truth has revealed itself, death brings us all to the threshold of what is most deeply human.

And it is there, in the silence and the sorrow, in the song and the prayer, in the ritual and the shared presence, that I have seen the face of dignity.

BEYOND TOLERANCE TO SACRED RECOGNITION

In our modern, multicultural healthcare environment, there is a commendable emphasis on tolerance and inclusion. Yet, what I have learned is that tolerance is not the final goal, *sacred recognition* is. It is not enough to simply make space for difference; we must learn to see difference as beautiful, sacred, and essential to the fullness of our shared humanity.

The Caribbean grandmother who cries silently, the Nigerian son who prays in tongues, the Muslim family who recites the Qur'an by the bedside, the Hindu daughter who offers sacred Ganges water, the Polish man who clutches his rosary with trembling hands, each of these is a unique and holy expression of the human spirit at the threshold of eternity. And chaplaincy, at its best, becomes the sacred space where all these expressions are received without dilution, judgement, or comparison.

We are not fixers. We are not gurus. We are not neutral. We are bridges, linking families with staff, connecting clinical realities with spiritual needs, interpreting between languages and meanings, and holding the delicate space between life and death.

We are witnesses, to last breaths, final blessings, reconciliations long hoped for, words spoken too late, and moments of quiet release. And we are learners, forever listening, forever adapting, forever seeking to understand.

Our presence is not merely professional, it is prophetic. We keep open the space where every person, whatever their background, can be seen, honoured, and accompanied with dignity to the very end.

To my fellow chaplains, especially those navigating the intersection of race, culture, and spiritual care: You belong in this work. Your voice matters. Your presence is powerful. Do not silence your story in the name of "professional neutrality." Let your difference be your gift, for it allows you to see and hear what others may miss.

To healthcare staff: Never underestimate the sacredness of the final moments. Your kindness, your patience, and your willingness to embrace cultural insight make an immeasurable difference to grieving families. You may not remember every patient, but they will remember you, and so will their loved ones.

And to you, the reader: May these stories remind you that death is not merely an ending. It is a mirror, a place where culture, spirit, memory, and mystery converge. Let us care for the dying in ways that honour their story, respond tenderly to their pain, and respect the uniqueness of their path. Because, in the end, what matters is not only *that* we die, but *how* we are accompanied when we do.

Dignity in diversity. That is the sacred calling.

APPENDICES

APPENDIX A: GLOSSARY OF CULTURAL AND RELIGIOUS END-OF-LIFE PRACTICES

This glossary provides a concise reference to common cultural and religious practices encountered at the end of life. While not exhaustive, it offers chaplains and healthcare staff a starting point for respectful and informed care.

Christianity

- **Prayer and Scripture Reading**: Common at the bedside; may include Psalms or the Lord's Prayer.

- **Anointing of the Sick / Last Rites**: Practiced in Catholicism and some Anglican traditions.

- **Worship Songs or Hymns**: Sometimes sung at the bedside or during transition.

- **Pastoral Presence**: The presence of a minister or chaplain is often seen as a sign of comfort and honour.

Islam

- **Shahada**: Declaration of faith often recited aloud or whispered into the ear of the dying person.

- **Facing Mecca**: It is preferred that the body be positioned to face Mecca.

- **Ritual Washing (Ghusl)**: Post-death body preparation is done by the same sex family/community member.

- **Quick Burial**: Burial should occur as soon as possible after death, ideally within 24 hours.

Hinduism

- **Mantra Chanting**: Family may chant prayers such as "Om Namah Shivaya."

- **Ganges Water**: Holy water from the River Ganges may be placed in the mouth of the dying.

- **Lamp and Incense**: Lighting a diya (lamp) is symbolic; some families request incense, though it may not be permitted in hospital settings.

- **Cremation**: Typically, within 24 hours; ritual performed by the eldest son.

Sikhism

- **Reading of Gurbani (Scripture)**: Recitation from the Guru Granth Sahib, especially *Japji Sahib*.

- **Waheguru Chant**: Repeated at the bedside to aid spiritual transition.

- **Uncut Hair and Articles of Faith**: Must be treated with utmost respect; removal is forbidden.

- **Cremation**: Preferred, usually accompanied by readings and hymns.

Judaism

- **Viddui**: A final confession or prayer recited by or for the dying person.

- **Presence of Family**: It's customary for family to be present and offer prayers.

- **Chevra Kadisha**: Sacred burial society responsible for body preparation.

- **Quick Burial**: Ideally within 24 hours; cremation generally discouraged.

African and Caribbean Traditions

- **Communal Gathering**: Extended family and community often gather for prayer and support.

- **Expressions of Grief**: May include weeping, singing, or testimonies.

- **Ancestral Language or Songs**: May be spoken or sung to accompany the dying.

- **Homegoing Service**: In Christian contexts, the funeral is viewed as a celebration of return to God.

APPENDIX B: NHS AND SPIRITUAL CARE GUIDANCE DOCUMENTS

Below is a summary of key NHS guidelines and frameworks relating to chaplaincy, spiritual care, and culturally sensitive end-of-life support.

1. NHS Chaplaincy Guidelines (NHS England)

- Emphasises the delivery of person-centred spiritual care to all patients, staff, and families, regardless of religious affiliation.

- Recognises spiritual care as essential to holistic care and patient wellbeing.

- Recommends regular chaplaincy presence, multi-faith representation, and support for staff wellbeing.

2. NHS Constitution for England

- Affirms the right of patients to receive care that respects their human rights, values, and beliefs.

- Supports compassionate, dignified, and culturally respectful care at the end of life.

3. National End of Life Care Strategy (Department of Health, 2008)

- Encourages spiritual care integration within multidisciplinary palliative care.

- Highlights the role of chaplains in supporting emotional and existential concerns.

4. Faith at End of Life: A Resource for Professionals (Public Health England)

- Offers practical guidance for accommodating different religious practices at end of life.

- Highlights communication tips and considerations for respectful practice.

5. Equality Act 2010

- Mandates that public services, including healthcare, must not discriminate on the basis of religion or belief.

- Upholds the duty to make reasonable accommodations for faith and cultural needs.

For detailed reading or to download up-dated documents, visit:

- https://www.england.nhs.uk

- https://www.gov.uk/government/pub-lications/faith-at-end-of-life

APPENDIX C: REFLECTION QUES-TIONS FOR CHAPLAINCY STUDENTS AND PRACTITIONERS

Use these questions for personal reflection, team discussion, or chaplaincy supervision. They are designed to deepen cultural aware-ness and spiritual sensitivity.

Reflecting on Practice

1. When did I last feel fully present with a patient from a different culture or faith? What made that possible?

2. Have I ever made assumptions about a patient's spirituality based on ethnicity or appearance? What was the outcome?

3. How do I respond internally when a patient's cultural expression is unfamiliar or uncomfortable for me?

Listening and Presence

4. How do I ensure that my listening is shaped more by curiosity than by correction?

5. What does silence mean in different cultures I encounter, and how do I respond to it?

Faith and Spiritual Tensions

6. How do I support families whose faith beliefs seem to conflict with medical advice?

7. What theological or pastoral language do I use that might need rethinking in a multi-faith environment?

Cultural Humility

8. What steps am I taking to move beyond cultural competence toward cultural humility?

9. When did I last allow a patient or family to teach me something about their worldview?

Self-Awareness

10. What are my own spiritual or cultural biases, and how might they affect my chaplaincy?

11. How do I look after my emotional and spiritual wellbeing in response to repeated exposure to death?

Team Integration

12. How do I communicate the value of spiritual care to clinical staff?

13. In what ways can I advocate for spiritual dignity in hospital protocols or ward culture?

Crossroads Of Culture and Care